The Girls' Christmas book

PSS!

PRICE STERN SLOAN

An Imprint of Penguin Group (USA) Inc.

Written by Ellen Bailey

Illustrated by Ann Kronheimer

Cover illustrated by Andrew Geeson

Use common sense at all times—always wear appropriate safety gear,
be very careful with scissors, and be considerate of other people.

PRICE STERN SLOAN
Published by the Penguin Group
Penguin Group (USA) Inc., 375 Hudson Street, New York, New York 10014, USA
Penguin Group (Canada), 90 Eglinton Avenue East, Suite 700,
Toronto, Ontario M4P 2Y3, Canada
(a division of Pearson Penguin Canada Inc.)
Penguin Books Ltd., 80 Strand, London WC2R 0RL, England
Penguin Group Ireland, 25 St. Stephen's Green, Dublin 2, Ireland
(a division of Penguin Books Ltd.)
Penguin Group (Australia), 250 Camberwell Road, Camberwell, Victoria 3124, Australia
(a division of Pearson Australia Group Pty. Ltd.)
Penguin Books India Pvt. Ltd., 11 Community Center,
Panchsheel Park, New Delhi—110 017, India
Penguin Group (NZ), 67 Apollo Drive, Rosedale, Auckland 0632, New Zealand
(a division of Pearson New Zealand Ltd.)
Penguin Books (South Africa) (Pty.) Ltd., 24 Sturdee Avenue,
Rosebank, Johannesburg 2196, South Africa

Penguin Books Ltd., Registered Offices:
80 Strand, London WC2R 0RL, England

Copyright © 2010, 2011 Buster Books. First published in Great Britain as *The Girls' Christmas Book* and *The Girls' Rainy Day Book*
by Buster Books, an imprint of Michael O'Mara Books Limited. First published in the United States in 2012 by
Price Stern Sloan, a division of Penguin Young Readers Group, 345 Hudson Street, New York, New York 10014.
PSS! is a registered trademark of Penguin Group (USA) Inc. Manufactured in Singapore.

ISBN 978-0-8431-7198-3   10 9 8 7 6 5 4 3 2 1

CONTENTS

Finish decorating the Christmas tree.

CHRISTMAS LISTS

There are so many things to look forward to at Christmas. Fill in these lists of your "Christmas top fives" to get you in the holiday spirit.

TOP 5 CHRISTMAS MOVIES

1. ....
2. ....
3. ....
4. ....
5. ....

TOP 5 CHRISTMAS FOODS

1. ....
2. ....
3. ....
4. ....
5. ....

TOP 5 CHRISTMAS SONGS

1. ....
2. ....
3. ....
4. ....
5. ....

TOP 5 CHRISTMAS GAMES

1. ....
2. ....
3. ....
4. ....
5. ....

TOP 5 CHRISTMAS GIFTS

1. ....
2. ....
3. ....
4. ....
5. ....

PUZZLE WORKSHOP

Complete the puzzles in Santa's busy workshop, and then turn to page 92 to find out the answers.

Can you spot seven differences between Santa Claus and his brother, Cornelius?

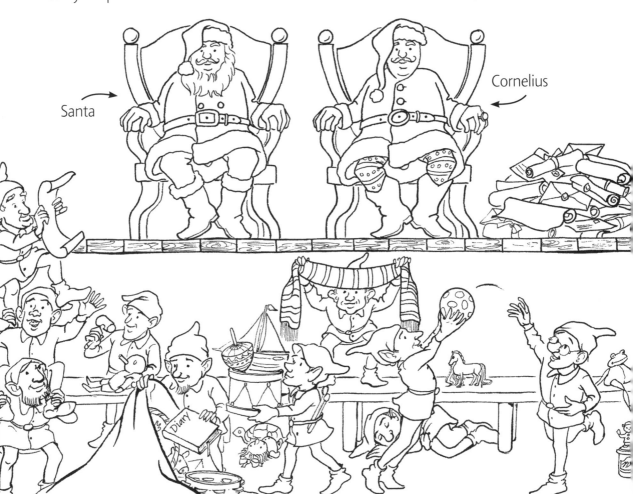

Santa

Cornelius

How many elves can you spot making mischief in Santa's workshop?

Which two reindeer are identical?

A B C D E F

The presents on this Christmas list are in the workshop somewhere. Can you find them all?

Dear Santa,

This year, I would like a diary, a necklace, a pony, a doll's house, and a scarf, please.

Love from Laura xxx

P.S. Merry Christmas!

MAKE YOUR BEDROOM A WINTER WONDERLAND

Follow these decorating tips to make your bedroom look as festive as you feel.

HOW ANGELIC!

Here's how to make a chain of pretty paper angels to hang in your room for that extra touch of Christmas magic.

1. Take an 11 x 17 in. piece of paper and cut it lengthways into three long strips, each 3 ½ in. wide.

2. Draw an angel shape like the one below on the left-hand end of the first strip, starting with the left wing. Make sure that the left wing, the top, and the bottom of the angel touch the edges of the paper.

3. Fold the strip of paper back along the right-hand side of the angel so that the right wing of the angel touches the fold.

4. Continue folding the paper back and forth in an accordian behind the angel.

5. Cut out the angel shape, leaving the folds intact where the angel's wings touch them so the chain doesn't break. Trim off any excess paper at the end of the strip.

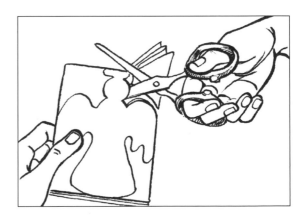

6. Unfold the paper to reveal your chain of angels. Make more angels from the remaining two strips of paper, then join them together with tape to make one chain. Why not hang your angels across the top of your bed or above your desk?

8

STUNNING SNOWFLAKES

Snowflakes are made of ice crystals that form beautiful, intricate patterns.
To create your own unique paper snowflake, you will need a square piece of
white paper at least 8 in. x 8 in. and a pair of scissors.

1. Fold the piece of paper in half diagonally to make a triangle, and crease it firmly.

2. Fold the triangle in half along the longest side again to create a smaller triangle.

3. Turn the triangle so that the longest side is at the top. Then fold the right-hand corner to just over halfway across the triangle.

5. Cut off the two points at the top of the triangle, so you are left with a flat edge at the top.

6. Now it's time to use some scissor skills. Cut shapes all around the edges of your triangle—smaller triangles, half circles, rectangles, squares and squiggles—the bigger and bolder the better.

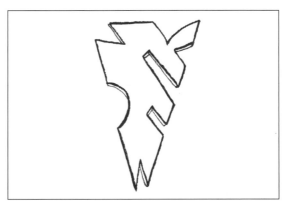

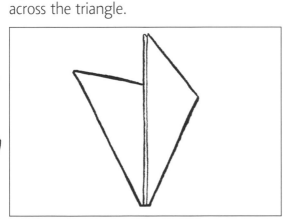

4. Now fold the other corner across so that its edge lines up with the far side of the triangle.

point → ← point

7. Unfold your finished snowflake and stick it to your window with tape. Make lots more using different-sized paper to create a flurry of gorgeous snowflakes that you'll see every time you open your curtains.

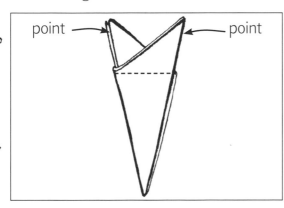

CREATE YOUR OWN CHRISTMAS TREE

Follow these steps to make a beautiful miniature Christmas tree for your room.

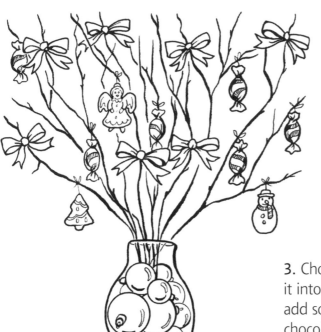

1. Fill a clear glass vase with bright Christmas ornaments—this will form the base for your Christmas tree.

2. Collect twigs or Christmas tree trimmings and carefully arrange them in the vase. Ask your parents for some small branches from the family Christmas tree if you have a real one.

3. Choose some pretty ribbon and tie it into bows on the branches. Why not add some foil-wrapped Christmas tree chocolates for a special touch?

CHRISTMAS TIPS

• String twinkling lights around your mirror to add some flair to your bedroom decorations.

• Drape tinsel over the tops of your picture frames, or attach it to your desk or bedside table with tape.

• Make a playlist of great Christmas tunes to get you in the festive mood. You could even have a Christmas sing-along with your friends.

GET YOUR SKATES ON

The girls want to ice-skate to the snowmen they have made. You can tell which girl made which snowman by the matching patterns on their scarves. The girls can skate straight up, down, and sideways, but not diagonally across the squares. Only one girl can pass through each square. Can you work out a path for each girl? The first one has been done for you. You can find the answers on page 92.

SNOWMEN TREATS

These tasty coconut snowmen are the perfect Christmas treats.

To make five snowmen, you will need:

- 2/3 cup condensed milk • 1 ½ cups shredded coconut
- 1 ⅔ cups powdered sugar + 3 ½ tablespoons extra
- 3 teaspoons water • raisins • red licorice strings

What you do:

1. Place a piece of parchment paper on a large plate.

2. Mix the condensed milk, coconut, and powdered sugar together in a bowl.

3. Dust some powdered sugar on your hands to stop the mixture from sticking, then roll it into five large balls for the bodies and five smaller balls for the heads.

4. Place the balls on a plate and put it in the fridge for five hours.

5. Mix the extra powdered sugar with three teaspoons of water to create a sugary paste.

6. Use the paste to stick the small balls on top of the larger balls to create five snowmen.

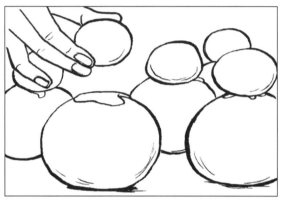

7. Use more of the paste to stick raisin eyes, mouths, and buttons onto the snowmen. Cut very small pieces out of red licorice to create noses. Then wrap longer pieces of licorice around the snowmen's necks for scarves. Your snowmen are ready to enjoy—yum!

WISH UPON A STAR

Inside each of the stars below, write a present that's on your ultimate Christmas wish list. When every star is filled in, see if you can draw another five-pointed star, bigger than all the other stars, that doesn't touch any of them. The solution is on page 92.

CHRISTMAS QUIZ

Test your Christmas knowledge with this festive quiz.
The answers are on page 93.

1. If you are born on Christmas Day what is your star sign?

A. Sagittarius

B. Aries

C. Libra

D. Capricorn

3. In "The Twelve Days of Christmas," how many ladies are dancing?

A. Six

B. Eight

C. Nine

D. Twelve

2. Where does Santa Claus live?

A. The North Pole

B. Antarctica

C. New Zealand

D. Russia

4. What color are holly berries?

A. Black

B. Blue

C. Red

D. Purple

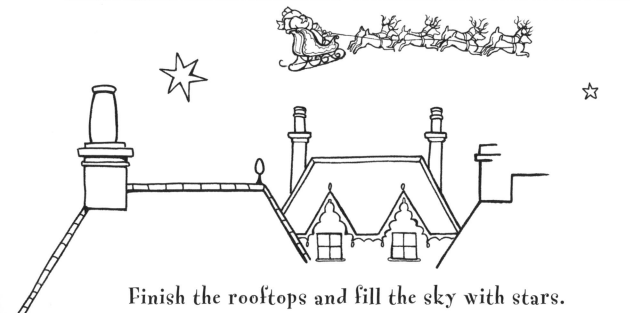

Finish the rooftops and fill the sky with stars.

5. Under which plant do people kiss at Christmas?

    A. Holly

    B. Mistletoe

    C. Ivy

    D. Fern

8. In which place was the first Christmas card sent?

    A. Australia

    B. England

    C. America

    D. Iceland

6. Which of the following is not one of Santa's reindeer?

    A. Dasher

    B. Dancer

    C. Vixen

    D. Mixie

9. Where was the composer of the popular carol "Silent Night" born?

    A. America

    B. France

    C. Austria

    D. Italy

7. What type of tree is a traditional Christmas tree?

    A. Oak

    B. Silver birch

    C. Fir

    D. Giant redwood

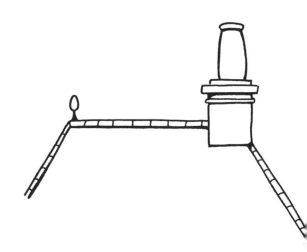

GO FISH!

Go Fish! is a card game for two to five players—perfect for a snowy day when you and your friends can't go out.

HOW TO PLAY

1. All you need is a deck of ordinary playing cards. Start by dealing seven cards to each player.

2. Spread out the remaining cards, facedown, on the floor or a table. This is your "pond." Each card is a "fish."

3. The goal of the game is to catch as many full sets of four fish as you can— for example, four twos, four eights, four kings and so on. The player to the left of the dealer goes first and asks one of the other players if they have any of the fish they are looking for:

"Katie, do you have any threes?"

4. If Katie has any of the requested cards, she must hand them over. If she doesn't have any, she tells the player to "Go fish!" That player must then take a card from the pond.

5. Continue playing around the circle to the left, following steps **3** and **4**. When a player collects four fish of the same value, she places them faceup in front of her on the floor or table.

6. If a player uses up all her cards on a turn, she fishes a card from the pond and play passes to the next player.

7. The game ends when all the cards have been used and all the sets of four fish have been completed. Whoever has made the most full sets wins.

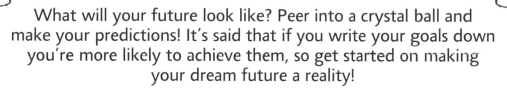

FUTURE FANTASTIC!

What will your future look like? Peer into a crystal ball and make your predictions! It's said that if you write your goals down you're more likely to achieve them, so get started on making your dream future a reality!

In ten years I will be a _____.

I will be living in _____ with _____.

My greatest achievement will be _____

_____.

I will be on my way to becoming a _____

_____.

My best friend will be _____ and

the thing we will most enjoy doing will be

_____.

CHRISTMAS SHOPPING CHAOS

Oh no! Sarah has left her shopping bags in the café.
Can you help her find her way through the maze of streets to
get them back? You will find the solution on page 93.

Decorate Santa's sleigh with some festive designs.

CHRISTMAS BEAUTY

Follow these top tips to give yourself some extra Christmas sparkle.

A FABULOUS RIBBON BARRETTE

Create a pretty, festive barrette using gift ribbon. Here's how . . .

1. Cut three 20 in. lengths of curling ribbon. With your thumb, hold the flat side of each piece of ribbon against the blade of an open pair of scissors.

2. Carefully scrape the scissors along the underside of the ribbon to create tight spirals.

3. Pinch the ribbons in the middle to create a crease and thread them onto a bobby pin so that the crease sits in the bend at the end of the pin. Tie a knot in each one to secure it around the bobby pin.

GLOWING SKIN

Keep your skin smooth and glowing for the party season.

Use a dry body brush on your whole body before you take a bath or shower. Use sweeping strokes, and always brush toward your heart. This will get rid of any dead cells and leave your skin supersoft. It will also improve your circulation and will make sure that you look your best!

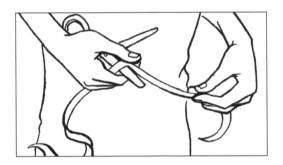

HONEY LIPS

Make your lips soft with a delicious homemade lip balm.

Find a small container to keep your lip balm in and wash it thoroughly with soap and water. Place three heaped teaspoons of petroleum jelly in a bowl, and add one large teaspoon of runny honey to it. Use the back of a spoon to mix it all together until it forms a smooth paste. Scoop the mixture into your lip-balm container and your honey-sweet lip balm is ready to go!

PERFECT PARTY HAIR

Create some Christmas curls with this glamorous hairstyle.

1. Comb your hair into a side part.

2. Spray lots of hairspray over your hair to prepare it for the style. Make sure you keep your eyes and mouth closed while you spray.

3. Curl your hair in small sections using rollers. Take a small section of hair and wrap it around the roller starting at the end. Roll it until you reach your head.

4. Spray your hair with hairspray again and remove the rollers. Your hair should now be in tight curls.

5. Gently brush out the curls to create luxurious waves.

6. Use bobby pins to loosely pin the front sections of your hair to the sides of your head above your ears.

7. Pin the gorgeous ribbon barrette (see opposite page) behind your ear for a fabulous finishing touch.

HOLIDAY HANDKERCHIEF

Snowy weather can ruin your hairdo, so wrap up
in a handkerchief to keep your locks looking perfect!

CLASSIC WRAP

1. Take a large, square handkerchief and fold it in half along the diagonal to create a triangle.

2. Place it over your head so that the middle of the folded side is in the center of your forehead and the tip is pointing down your back.

3. Take the two ends and tie them in a knot at the back of your head under your hair.

4. Push the front of the handkerchief back above your hairline for a softer look.

GYPSY CHIC

1. Hold a long scarf over your head so that the middle of one of the long sides is flat against your forehead.

2. Gather the scarf at the nape of your neck, then twist it around all the way to the bottom.

3. Tie a knot in the scarf at the nape of your neck, then pull the length of it forward over your shoulder.

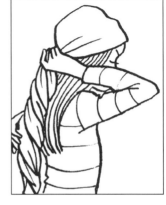

4. Accessorize with some large hoop earrings to complete the gypsy look.

ARABIAN DREAM

1. Tip your head forward and hold a long scarf over your head so that the middle of one of the long sides is flat against the nape of your neck.

2. Gather the fabric at your forehead and twist it all the way to the bottom.

3. Lift your head up and take the twisted fabric back over your head and around one side. Then pull it forward over the opposite shoulder.

4. Accessorize with lots of sparkly bangles.

VINTAGE QUEEN

1. Take a square handkerchief and fold it in half to create a triangle.

2. Hold the handkerchief across your shoulders so that the tip is pointing down your back and the straight edge is underneath your hair.

3. Pick up the two ends and tie them in a knot on top of your head.

4. Pull the point of the handkerchief up over your head, tucking long hair away inside, then slip the end of the handkerchief under the front of the knot.

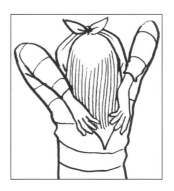

5. Tie the ends in a second knot to ensure the point stays in place, then tuck the ends in too.

6. Wear with a striped sailor top to complete the look.

A GENIUS GIFT

Here's how to turn an
ordinary notebook into
a stylish denim notebook.

You will need:

- an old pair of jeans (check with an adult that it's okay for you
to use them) • a pair of scissors • a blank notebook • a pen
• strong, all-purpose glue • roughly 3 ft. of wide ribbon

What you do:

1. First cut the legs off the jeans so that you have two tubes of fabric. Then cut along the inside seams of one of the legs so that you have a piece of denim with a seam down the center.

2. Lay the denim flat on a table with the wrong side facing up. Open the book on top of the piece of fabric so that the seam runs horizontally across the middle of the cover. Use the pen to draw around it.

3. Draw another rectangle about 1 ¼ in. larger around the one you've just drawn. Then cut along this outside line.

4. Cover the front of the book with glue, then stick the fabric to it, matching up the edges of the book with the inner rectangle drawn on the fabric. Repeat for the back cover.

5. Cut a diagonal line across the corners and in the middle at the top and bottom of the fabric as shown below.

6. Spread a thin line of glue around the three outer edges of the inside front cover of the book. Then fold the edges of the fabric in and stick them down. Repeat for the back cover.

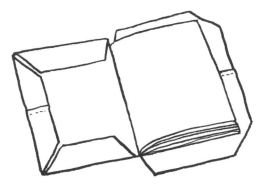

7. Cut your length of ribbon in half and add a dab of glue to the end of one piece. Stick it to the inside edge of the front cover. Repeat for the back cover and leave to dry.

Top Tip: If your length of ribbon has a wrong side and a right side, glue the right side to the inside covers, so that it shows when you close your note book.

8. Cut carefully around one of the back pockets of your jeans. You should now have a denim pocket with two layers of fabric. Cover the back of the pocket with glue, then stick it to the front of your notebook. Leave to dry.

In-jean-ious!

Decorate her coat and boots.

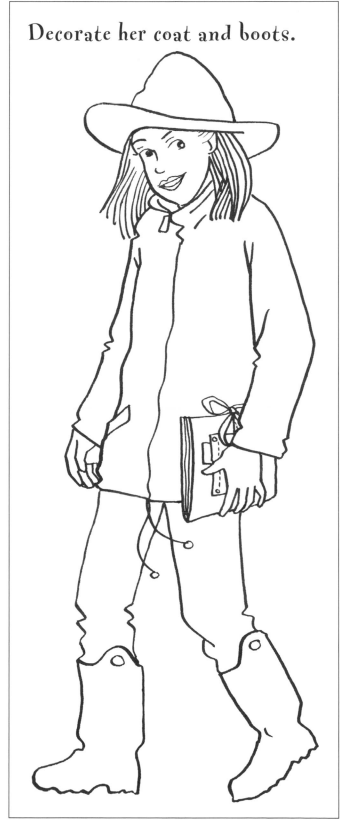

PERFECT POM-POMS

Brighten up any Christmas tree with beautiful pom-pom decorations. Follow these steps to make them.

You will need:

• thick cardboard • pair of compasses • a marker or pen • scissors • five 6 ½ ft. lengths of red, white, or yellow yarn • 12 in. length of black yarn

What you do:

1. Use the compasses to draw two circles measuring 2 in. across on the cardboard. Draw smaller circles measuring ¾ in. across in the middle of each one and cut them out, making two ring shapes. Ask an adult to help you with this part.

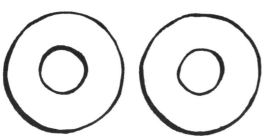

2. Place the two cardboard rings together and wind one of the lengths of yarn around them, as shown.

3. When you reach the end of a piece of yarn, start winding the next piece of yarn around the rings from the point the last piece ended. Make sure the loose end is quickly covered as you wrap so that it doesn't come undone.

4. Wind all your yarn around the rings, overlapping several times, until the hole in the middle is so small that you can't push the yarn through anymore.

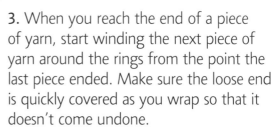

5. Push the tip of the blade of your scissors through the yarn where the circles of cardboard meet. Then cut all the way around the edges of the rings, taking care to cut through every single strand of yarn.

26

Once you've done this, your pom-pom will look like this:

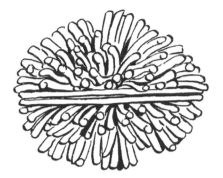

7. Carefully pull the two pieces of cardboard off the pom-pom.

8. Tie the black yarn tails that are sticking out of the top of the pom-pom in a loop and hang it on your Christmas tree.

6. Pull the two pieces of cardboard apart slightly and wrap the piece of black yarn around all the strands of yarn in the middle. Tie it in a tight knot, and cut it 4 in. away from the knot on either side, leaving two tails.

Cover the trees in pretty pom-poms.

WHAT'S YOUR CHRISTMAS SHOPPING STYLE?

Follow this fun flowchart to find out.

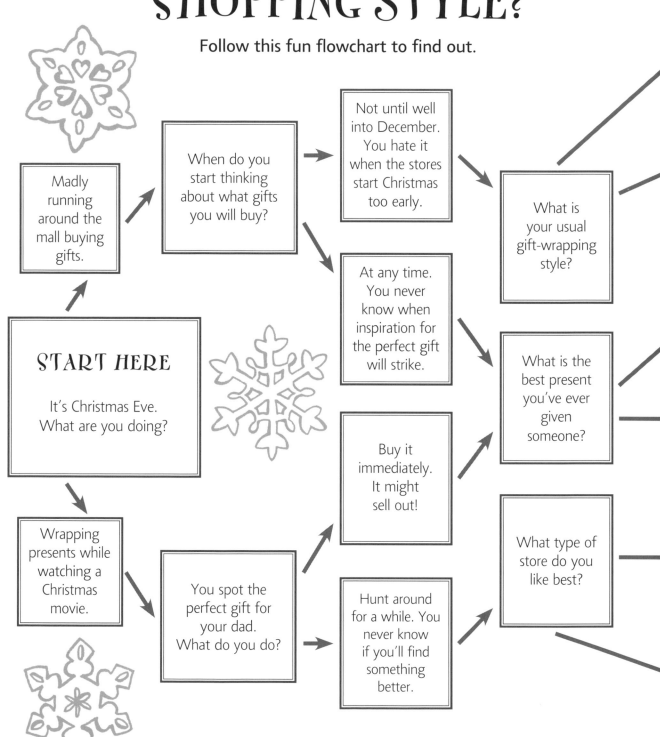

Madly running around the mall buying gifts.

When do you start thinking about what gifts you will buy?

Not until well into December. You hate it when the stores start Christmas too early.

What is your usual gift-wrapping style?

START HERE

It's Christmas Eve. What are you doing?

At any time. You never know when inspiration for the perfect gift will strike.

What is the best present you've ever given someone?

Buy it immediately. It might sell out!

Wrapping presents while watching a Christmas movie.

You spot the perfect gift for your dad. What do you do?

Hunt around for a while. You never know if you'll find something better.

What type of store do you like best?

Simple. You're happy to put your presents in gift bags or wrap them in tissue.

Stunning. To you, the wrapping is as important as the gift inside.

Something you know they had been looking for for ages.

A gift you made yourself and put lots of time and effort into.

A craft shop where you can buy the things you need to make your gifts.

A department store where you can get everything you need in one try.

LAID-BACK LADY

You don't enjoy making lists or planning and prefer to leave everything to the last minute. It's great that you're so relaxed about Christmas, but the more effort you put into buying your gifts, the more fun you'll get out of giving them.

FAB FRIEND

Your friends and family always look forward to receiving gifts from you, because they know how carefully you think about what they'd like. You remember conversations about the things they love and use this to get thoughtful, personal gifts.

CREATIVE CHICK

You're awesome at making beautiful gifts, and the little touches that you add are always perfect. Everyone cherishes the gifts you give them because they know they've been made with love and attention. Don't forget to make something for yourself when Christmas is over.

SAVVY SHOPPER

You are superorganized and like to have lists of what you're going to give people. You always have your shopping finished by the second week of December. Santa would be lucky to have you on his team!

TRICKY TRACKS

A naughty elf has opened the stable doors and some of the reindeer have escaped! Can you help Santa put them back by following the tracks in the snow to work out which reindeer is which?

Turn to page 93 to find the answers.

PRANCER   DANCER   DASHER   COMET   CUPID

Christmas is celebrated all over the world.
Complete the snowman in the snow . . .

. . . and decorate the sand tree
in the sunshine.

BRAIN BOGGLERS

See how quickly you can complete these logic puzzles without your brain exploding! Record how long it takes you to figure out each one in the spaces provided. You'll find the answers on pages 93 and 94.

TROPHY TIME

Three friends, Emily, Alyssa, and Preeya, are discussing how many football trophies a boy in their class, named Alex, has won. Only one of them is correct—the other two are wrong. Can you figure out who by studying their conversation?

"Alex is so sweet, and he's won more than one football trophy," said Emily.

"He's won at least five!" Alyssa scoffed.

Preeya interrupted, saying, "I heard that it's an even number."

How many trophies has Alex won?

Time: . . . .

Answer: . . . .

SUNFLOWER SUMS

Alice is growing a sunflower that doubles in height every day. After 30 days, the sunflower will be as tall as she is. After how many days would the sunflower be half her height?

Time: . . . .

Answer: . . . .

SUMMER FUN

Summer's mom has four children. The first child is called April, the second child is called May, and the third child is called June. What is the name of the fourth child?

Time: . . . .

Answer: . . . .

DONKEY DILEMMA

Can you move just one toothpick to make the donkey change position?

Time: . . . .

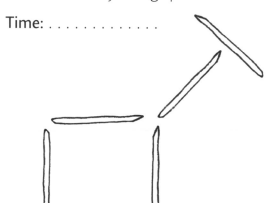

CHOCOLATE CONUNDRUM

Rebecca has bought three boxes of chocolates for her friends: white chocolates for Kate, milk chocolates for Sarah, and a mixture of milk and white chocolates for Bella. However, the chocolate labels have been mixed up, and the boxes all look the same! None of the labels are correct.

Rebecca thinks she can shake a chocolate out of one box without tearing it, but how could she work out which label goes on which box by taking just one chocolate from one box?

Time: . . . .   Answer: . . . .

WHO'S THE TOP?

Four friends are trying to decide who is the tallest—can you work it out just from these clues?

Louisa is only taller than Siân and Preeya is shorter than Sally. However, Preeya is taller than Siân, and Sally is taller than Louisa.

How tall are they? Check one box for each of them.

Time: . . . .

	3 ft. 3 in.	3 ft. 5 in.	3 ft. 7 in.	3 ft. 9 in.
Louisa				
Siân				
Sally				
Preeya				

THE MAGIC SNOW GLOBE

Maisy sat at the end of her bed and tore open the gift that Aunt Beth had sent her. A snow globe and a piece of crinkled brown paper fell into her lap. On the paper was written, "Shake three times, then make a wish." She peered inside the globe and saw a tiny model village with a large Christmas tree. She shook the snow globe and watched as the sparkling snow fell onto the rooftops. She shook the globe twice more and said, "I wish I was somewhere snowy."

A dazzling light filled Maisy's room and suddenly she found herself sitting on a bench covered in snow. She saw a huge Christmas tree up ahead and ran toward it. The tree was beautiful, and there were pretty houses and stores along the street. Maisy couldn't see anyone around, but she wasn't worried—soon enough she was sure to see someone who would tell her how to get home.

Maisy began building a huge snowman. By the time she had finished, she was tired and hungry, but still she hadn't seen a single person. She knocked on the door of every house, but not a single door opened. The town was deserted. She ran back to the snowman and threw herself down in front of him. "What should I do?" she cried. "I want to go home."

"You need a snow key," said a deep voice. Maisy looked up at the snowman in surprise. "Don't be afraid," he continued. "Walk over there. You'll come to the edge of my world and be able to look at your own, but you must make a snow key to get out."

Maisy ran in the direction the snowman had pointed and sure enough, she hit a great, glass wall. Looking out of it, she could see a giant version of her bedroom. She gasped as she realized that she was **inside** the snow globe!

Suddenly she saw a keyhole. She remembered what the snowman had told her, so she picked up some snow, squashed it into a key shape, then put it into the hole. With a flash of light, Maisy tumbled back into her bedroom.

When she looked into the snow globe she could see a snowman and some fresh, snowy footprints that she was sure hadn't been there when she'd unwrapped her gift.

MAKE A SNOW SHAKER

Make a snow shaker and guarantee you'll have a white Christmas—even if there's no chance of snow! You might even have an adventure like Maisy's . . .

You will need:

• glass jar with a watertight lid • clear putty
• plastic Christmas toy or cake decoration that will fit inside the jar
• glycerin (a syrupy liquid found at drug stores and in the home baking aisle in supermarkets) • water • silver glitter • ribbon

What you do:

1. Stick a lump of clear putty to the inside of the jar's lid. Leave a gap around the sides of the lid so that you'll be able to screw it back onto the jar later on.

2. Stick the plastic toy into the middle of the putty. Make sure it is firmly held in place so that it won't move when shaken or held upside down.

3. Mix equal parts of glycerin and water in a bowl. The mixture will be thicker than water, so when you add the glitter it will move more slowly within the liquid.

4. Pour the mixture into the jam jar and add the glitter. Screw the lid back on tightly, taking care not to dislodge the toy from the putty.

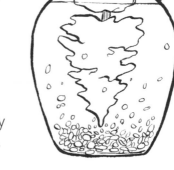

5. Tie the ribbon around the top of the jar to hide the lid.

6. Turn the jar upside down and watch as the glittery snow falls slowly over the festive scene inside.

IT'S A BIRDIE!

This little bird makes such a cute present that you might want to give it to yourself!

You will need:

• a pencil • a piece of paper • a sharp pair of scissors • a piece of fabric about the size of this page (Try to choose a fabric that doesn't fray easily, such as felt.) • pins • a needle and thread • 2 buttons • a pair of old socks

What to do:

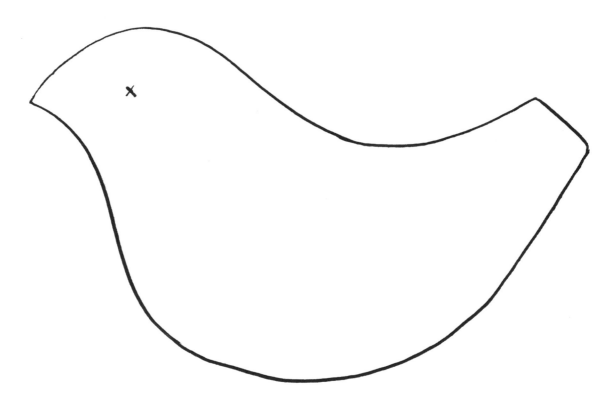

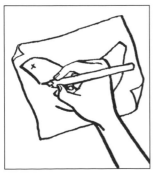

1. Trace over the picture of the bird above and cut it out. This is your template.

2. Fold the large piece of fabric in half with the

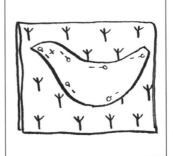

printed side on the outside if patterned.

3. Pin the paper bird on to the fabric as shown here.

36

4. Carefully cut around the edge of the paper bird so that you end up with two matching fabric birds. Unpin the template.

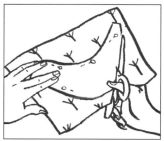

5. It's now time to sew some button eyes onto the fabric birds. Take a piece of thread the length of your arm and thread the needle. Pull the thread halfway through, then tie the ends in a double knot.

6. Place one of the buttons on the printed side of one of the fabric birds where its eye would be (marked with an X opposite).

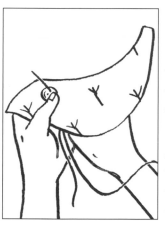

7. From below, push the needle up through the fabric and through one of the holes in the button. Pull it all the way through until the knot hits the fabric.

8. Push the needle down into the next hole and continue passing the needle up and down through the fabric and buttonholes until the button is secure.

9. Finish with the needle on the non-printed side of the fabric and secure it with a double knot. Trim the thread.

10. Sew the second button on to the other bird-shaped piece of fabric in the same way.

11. Pin the two bird-shaped pieces of fabric together so the printed sides face outward.

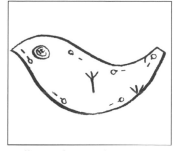

12. Thread the needle with another piece of thread about the length of your arm. Push the needle through the fabric about ¼ in. from the edge.

13. Bring the needle back up through the fabric about ⅛ in. to the right of the first hole. Make several stitches on this spot to secure the thread.

14. Push the needle up and down through the fabric, making stitches that are ⅛ in. long.

15. Continue sewing around the bird until just a ¾ in. hole is left.

16. Cut the socks into pieces, then push the pieces through the hole to stuff the bird.

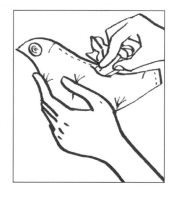

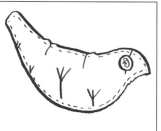

17. Sew the hole closed, then tie the end of the thread in a knot and cut off the excess.

Hint: Why not add a loop of ribbon, so that you can hang your birdie up?

CHRISTMAS GREETINGS

Christmas is celebrated by millions of people all over the world. Become an international Christmas queen, and learn to say "Merry Christmas" in several different languages.

A guide showing how to pronounce the words is shown in italics.

FRENCH

Joyeux Noël

Jwa-yeuh No-elle

HAWAIIAN

Mele Kalikimaka

Me-leh Ka-lee-kee-ma-kah

FINNISH

Hyvää Joulua

Hi-vah Yo-lu-ah

SPANISH

Feliz Navidad

Fay-leese Na-vee-dahd

GERMAN

Fröhliche Weihnachten

Froh-lic-uh Vy-nac-ten

ITALIAN

Buon Natale

Bwon Na-tal-eh

HOT CHOCOLATE HEAVEN

When it's dark outside and there's a chill in the air, there's nothing more cozy than a mug of hot chocolate.

You will need:

- 1¾ cups superfine sugar • 2 ¾ cups cocoa powder
- enough milk to fill a mug • 10 miniature marshmallows

What you do:

1. Mix the sugar and cocoa powder in a large mixing bowl using a whisk.

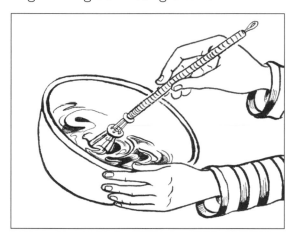

2. Place two heaping tablespoons of the mixture into a mug.

3. Pour the milk into a saucepan, and heat it on the stove until it's just starting to boil. Ask an adult to help you with this.

4. Turn off the heat, and carefully pour the hot milk into your mug. Ask an adult to help you.

5. Give the hot chocolate a good stir until the mixture has dissolved.

6. Sprinkle marshmallows on top.

7. Place the remaining mix into a storage container, so you can whip up a delicious cup of hot chocolate all through the Christmas holidays.

Christmas Tip:

Instead of a spoon, why not use a candy cane to stir your hot chocolate?

It's sure to add a minty zing to your cup.

WET WEATHER WISHES

When the weather outside is frightful, it's time to decide whether you'd rather splash around in puddles and snowdrifts or curl up with a good book.

If it is raining outside, I am more likely to . . .

. . . be happy—I love the rain! ☐

. . . hope for a rainbow. ☐

. . . feel miserable. ☐

. . . have fun indoors. ☐

The last thing I want to do when it snows is . . .

. . . let it change my plans. ☐

. . . go outside. ☐

. . . get wet feet. ☐

. . . stay at home. ☐

The best thing to do if I am out in the rain is . . .

. . . splash in the puddles! ☐

. . . drink raindrops. ☐

. . . spin my umbrella. ☐

. . . have a water fight. ☐

When the weather is snowy, I'd rather be . . .

. . . shopping with my friends. ☐

. . . playing in the park. ☐

. . . riding my bike. ☐

. . . reading in the sun. ☐

If it's raining, my parents are most likely to say . . .

. . . "It's good for the plants." ☐

. . . "Do some homework." ☐

. . . "Help me around the house." ☐

. . . "Play outside, anyway." ☐

On a snowy day, the best thing to do indoors is . . .

. . . imagine I'm somewhere warm. ☐

. . . play with my family. ☐

. . . watch a DVD. ☐

. . . curl up with a good book. ☐

MAJOR MIX-UP

The pieces of this jigsaw puzzle have gotten mixed up with some pieces from another jigsaw puzzle. Can you work out which three pieces fit in the spaces? The answers are on page 94.

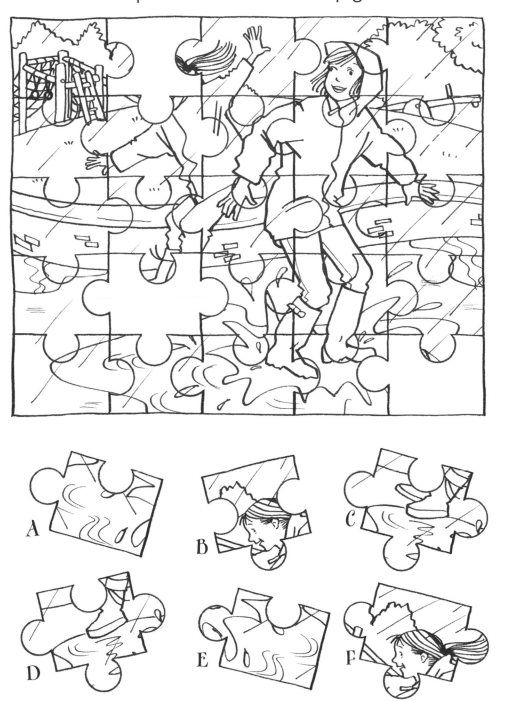

CLASSIC CHRISTMAS GAMES

You've opened the presents and you're full of delicious Christmas dinner. Now it's time to make sure the fun continues with these festive family games.

FAMOUS FOREHEADS

1. Ask each player to write the name of a famous person on a sticky note and stick it on another player's forehead so everyone else can see the name aside from that player. The player then "becomes" this person, even though they don't know who they are yet.

2. Ask the youngest player to go first. They must ask a question about who they are to the rest of the group. The question can only be answered with a yes or no. They might ask something like, "Am I a girl?" or, "Am I a singer?" If the answer is yes then the player gets another turn. If the answer is no, play moves clockwise to the next person.

3. The first person to correctly guess who they are wins the game. Play continues until everyone has guessed who they are.

PICTURE ROUND

This is a game that you can prepare for your friends and family to play. Here's how to make it:

1. Flip through magazines and cut out pictures of famous people, places, or objects.

2. Stick all the pictures onto a sheet of paper and number each one.

3. Provide each player with a piece of paper and a pencil and instruct them to identify as many of the pictures as they can.

4. Collect all the answer sheets, then count up how many each player got right and announce the winner.

READY, STEADY, DRAW!

For this game, you will need two teams of at least two people, a large bowl, a timer, paper, and a pen.

1. Ask each player to write the names of six objects on small pieces of paper. Then ask them to fold up their pieces of paper and place them in the bowl.

2. Decide which team is going to go first and set the timer for one minute.

3. The first player on the team picks a piece of paper out of the bowl. The player must then draw the object while their team guesses what they are drawing. As soon as one of their teammates guesses what it is, the

player puts the piece of paper on the floor and takes a new name from the bowl. The player must try to draw as many objects as they can in one minute.

4. When the time's up, the first player on the other team has one minute to draw as many objects as they can while their teammates guess. The second player on the first team then has a turn, and so on, until all the pieces of paper have been taken from the bowl.

5. Count up how many objects each team has guessed correctly. The winning team can then choose a task for the losing team—such as doing all the Christmas cleaning up!

HOPPING ORIGAMI

Make an origami frog that really hops! You can then use it as a counter for the lily pad game on the next page. All you need is a square of froggy-green paper.

1. First, fold the piece of paper in half.

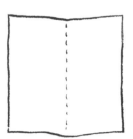

the two sides together so that they meet in the middle.

2. Fold the top-left corner down so that the top of the paper lines up with the right-hand side. Then unfold it again.

The top of the paper will now fold down to form a triangle, like this:

3. Now fold the top-right corner down so that the top of the paper lines up with the left-hand side. Then unfold it again.

6. Fold the bottom of the paper up so that the edge lines up with the bottom of the triangle.

4. Turn the paper over and fold down the top at the point where the diagonal creases meet to make a horizontal crease as shown here.

7. Fold the corners at the bottom of the triangle up to make the frog's front legs.

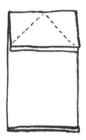
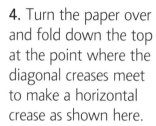

5. Unfold the paper again and hold it by the edges of the horizontal line. Bring

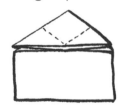

8. Next, fold in the straight sides so that they meet in the middle.

9. Fold the straight sides up so that they reach the bottom of the frog's legs. Unfold them again, leaving a crease.

10. Reach under the flaps at the bottom with your thumbs, holding the middle in place with your fingers. Pull the flaps upward and outward into points so that the lower edge comes up to reach the bottom of the frog's legs.

Note: If you would like to make frog counters to play Lilypad Hoppers (see page 46), start with a square of paper measuring roughly 4 in. across. Use a different shade for each player.

11. Fold the points down so that they meet at the bottom as shown here.

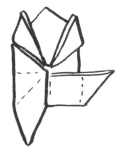 

12. Now fold these points out diagonally to make your frog's back legs.

13. Next, fold your frog in half across the middle, then fold the back legs back again in a zigzag so that the frog's back legs will be underneath its body.

14. That's it! Turn your frog over. To make it hop, press and flick on its back. You can use your frog for a game of Lilypad Hoppers on the next page.

LILYPAD HOPPERS

Race your friends across the pond and be the first to make it to the riverbank on the other side!

First, get each of your friends to make an origami frog as a counter (see pages 44 and 45). Alternatively, use a different coin each instead. Place the frogs at the start, then take turns spinning the spinner (follow the instructions opposite to get spinning) and move forward the number of spaces shown.

You stop to look at some tadpoles. Miss a turn.

Take a shortcut across the stepping stones.

START HERE

A gnome points you in the wrong direction. Move back 3 spaces.

Slide down the swan's neck to move ahead 2 spaces.

Miss a turn while you feed the fish.

You get a boost from a snack of flies—move on 1 space.

SPINNER

1 2 3 4 5 6

Cut around the dotted line and pierce the middle of your spinner with a toothpick.

To spin, hold the toothpick upright on the playing surface and spin it between your thumb and forefinger. When the spinning stops, the number at the top is the number of lily pads your frog is allowed to hop.

Take a shortcut down the waterfall.

You catch a ride on a dragonfly. Move forward 3 spaces.

A duck steals your breakfast. Miss a turn.

GOOD HOPPING!

FINISH HERE

You stop to make a crown of lilies. Miss a turn.

Everyone else's lily pads sink—they all miss a turn!

Your feet get tangled in reeds. Move back 3 spaces.

WHITE CHRISTMAS

It's a white Christmas and everything is covered in snow! Complete these wintry puzzles then turn to page 94 for the answers.

Who threw that? Follow the trails to work out which red-faced girl's snowball hit Aunt Sally.

Shade all the shapes with a dot in them to reveal a Christmas surprise.

Lydia has made a snowman. He has lumps of coal for buttons, but he doesn't have a carrot for a nose. He has a scarf but no hat.

Can you spot which of these is Lydia's snowman?

Decorate the Ice Queen's dress with snowy sparkles.

FRIENDOMETER

Each description below is worth a certain number of Friendship Points. Read each one, and if the sentence describes you perfectly, you can shade in the number of points shown, starting from the bottom of your Friendometer. How close to the top can you get?

HOW GOOD A FRIEND ARE YOU?

• I don't get jealous if my friends are friends with other people.
4 Friendship Points

• A friend can tell me if she's feeling worried.
2 Friendship Points

• I always remember my friends' birthdays.
2 Friendship Points

• I would help a friend with homework.
2 Friendship Points

• I like to make little gifts for my friends.
2 Friendship Points

• I'd lend a friend my prettiest shirt.
1 Friendship Point

• I often give my friends compliments.
2 Friendship Points

• My friends describe me as trustworthy.
2 Friendship Points

• I don't talk about friends behind their backs.
3 Friendship Points

• I've never broken a promise to a friend.
4 Friendship Points

• I would give a friend my last piece of candy.
1 Friendship Point

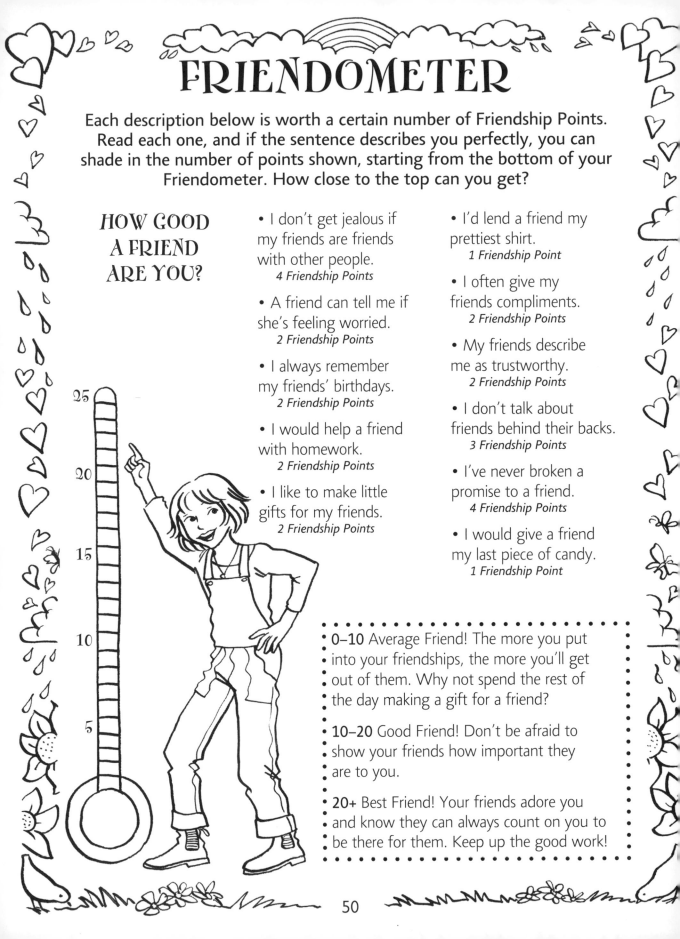

0–10 Average Friend! The more you put into your friendships, the more you'll get out of them. Why not spend the rest of the day making a gift for a friend?

10–20 Good Friend! Don't be afraid to show your friends how important they are to you.

20+ Best Friend! Your friends adore you and know they can always count on you to be there for them. Keep up the good work!

Decorate the lollipops and draw your own.

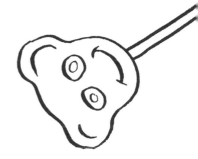

TRUE OR FALSE?

There are some weird and wonderful Christmas traditions around the world! Color these ornaments in green if you think they're true and red if you think they're false, then find the answers on page 94.

Ukrainians believe that finding a spider's web on Christmas Eve is good luck.

Spanish children play on swings at Christmas to tell the sun to "swing" high in the sky over the coming year.

Italian children are brought gifts by a friendly witch as well as Santa Claus.

At Christmas time, Swedish boys dress up as holly sprigs in bright-green clothes and red hats.

In Brazil, Santa wears red and white shorts so that he can enjoy the summer heat.

In Australia, Santa arrives on the back of a kangaroo.

PICTURE PERFECT

Use the grid lines to help you to draw your own version of this cute Christmas puppy in the box below.

PLAY THE CHESHIRE CAT

The Cheshire Cat is known for his mischievous grin, and getting people to smile is the aim of this game! Can you keep a straight face? Here's how to play:

1. A group of people sit in a circle with one person in the middle.

2. The person in the middle is the Cheshire Cat. Her job is to walk around on her hands and knees, purring and behaving like a cat in order to make the other players smile.

3. The Cheshire Cat should go up to each of the players in turn and say in a catlike voice, "Smile if you love me."

The player must then respond, "I do love you, Kitty, but I just can't smile."

4. If any of the players smile at any point, whether she is talking to the Cheshire Cat or not, she becomes the Cat and must swap places with the person in the middle of the circle.

5. If none of the players smile, then the person in the middle continues going around asking everyone until she manages to get someone to smile.

PICTURE THIS!

Using the grid lines to help you, draw your own version of
this picture in the bigger grid below with pens or pencils.

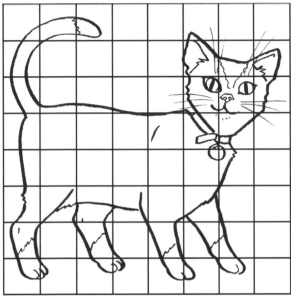

FROSTED GINGERBREAD COOKIES

These delicious gingerbread house cookies have a real Christmas crunch. You can have fun decorating them with your friends.

For 10 small houses you will need:

- ½ a beaten egg • 4 tablespoons unsalted butter
- ½ cup superfine sugar
- 1 ¼ cups flour
- ½ teaspoon allspice • ½ teaspoon ground cinnamon
- ½ teaspoon ground ginger

For the icing: • ⅔ cup powdered sugar
- 2 or 3 tablespoons warm water • sweets of your choice

What you do:

1. Mix together the egg, butter, and sugar with a wooden spoon until it is smooth.

2. Use a sieve to combine the flour and spices into the mixture and mix thoroughly with your hands. You should now have a soft dough. Add a little water if it is too dry or flour if it is too wet.

3. Cover the dough in plastic wrap and place it in the fridge for 30 minutes.

4. Heat the oven to 350°F and line a baking tray with parchment paper.

5. Sprinkle some flour onto a clean kitchen counter and use a rolling pin to roll out the dough until it is ¼ in. thick.

6. Using a cookie cutter or sharp knife, cut simple house-shapes out of the dough and place them on the baking tray.

7. Bake the cookies in the oven for 25–30 minutes until they are golden brown.

8. Once the cookies have cooled, mix together the powdered sugar and warm water to form a sugary paste.

9. Spread a thin layer of the paste onto the roof of each house and above the windows and doors for a snowy effect.

10. Add sweets to the paste while it is still wet—these will be your houses' twinkly Christmas lights.

Warning: Always ask an adult to help you when using sharp knives and a hot oven.

Decorate these cookie cottages with snow and sweets.

COOKIE MIX-UP

Emma has made some Christmas cookies and written words on them, but the letters are all jumbled up! Can you rearrange them to spell the words correctly? Turn to page 95 to find the answers.

1. CPAEE

2. OYJ

3. TAPYR

4. RMREY

5. VSIEETP

6. LMEIS

7. HIWS

8. YHPAP

A CHRISTMAS RESCUE

Read on to discover the heartwarming true story of a town in Canada that came together at Christmas to save some stranded horses.

It was a week before Christmas, and Logan Jeck was driving a snowmobile through the mountains near his home in Robson Valley, Canada.

Up ahead, he could see two animals. He was shocked as he approached them. "They were sick, starving horses," he remembers. They had been trapped by the snow and were on the verge of death.

Logan rushed home and told his dad and sister what he had seen. Together, they discussed the best way to get the horses down from their snowy prison. They considered harnessing the animals to a helicopter, pulling them on sleds, or even fitting them with special snowshoes, but none of these suggestions would work.

The only way to rescue the horses was to dig a long passageway through the towering snowdrifts. Logan and his sister, Toni, spread the word through the town about the poor, desperate horses.

It had been a difficult year in Robson Valley, and many people had lost their jobs. People were struggling with Christmas preparations, and it was one of the harshest winters they had seen in years. Despite all this, volunteers began to come forward to help dig a passageway that would save the horses' lives.

Soon, almost all the townsfolk were helping to dig the path through the snow. Finally, just two days before Christmas, the rescuers reached the horses and helped them trek for seven hours down the mountain to safety.

Many of the residents hadn't had time to put up Christmas trees or buy any presents. "But this still seems like the best Christmas ever," said one of them. "You realize these are the most important things in life—to help something that needs help."

PUPPY POWER!

Can you work out which puppy belongs to which girl?
The answers are on page 95.

Rosie

C

Leila

B

A

Caitlin

BUSY BEES

Busy Bees is a game for two players. Be the first to form a connected path of honey from one side of the hive to the other.

To play, you will need a red pen and a blue pen. Take turns coloring the hexagons on the board to the right.

Player **A** must try to create a linked path from the top left to the bottom right of the hive. Player **B** must try to create a linked path from the top right to the bottom left of the hive.

SNEAKY BEES

You can use sneaky bee tactics and use your turn to block your opponent.

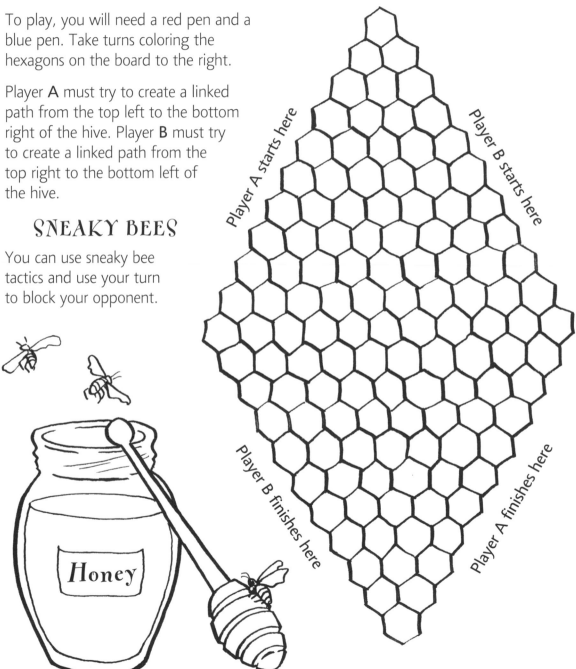

Player A starts here

Player B starts here

Player B finishes here

Player A finishes here

Honey

Decorate the stockings and hang more above the fireplace.

SHOP SUDOKU

A friend is working in a department store during the Christmas season and she asks you to arrange the window displays.

Complete the windows so that the columns, rows, and four larger squares each contain only one of the items listed at the bottom of that window. Answers are on page 95.

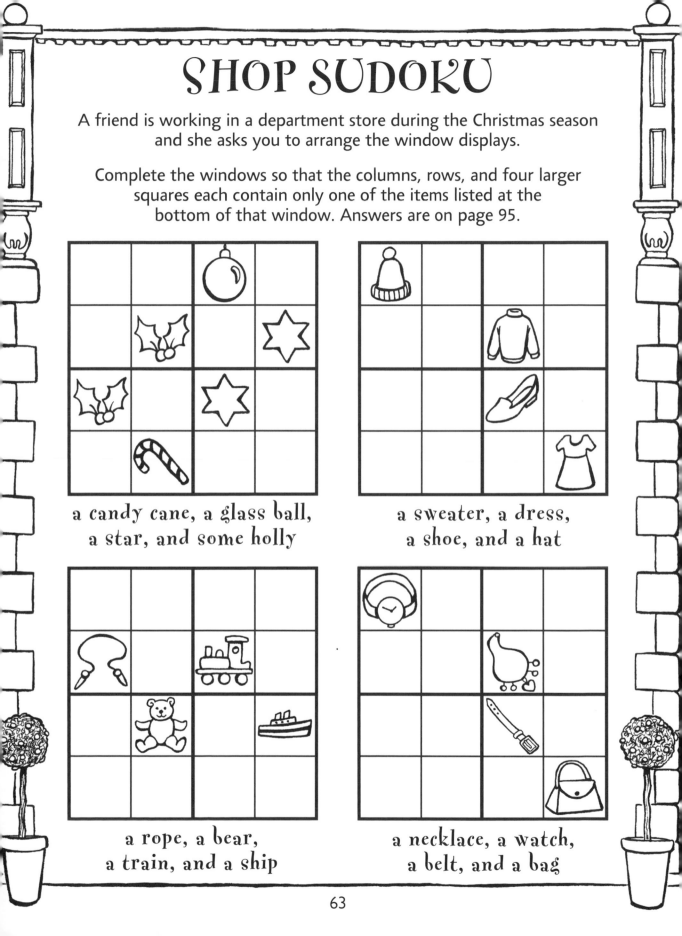

a candy cane, a glass ball,
a star, and some holly

a sweater, a dress,
a shoe, and a hat

a rope, a bear,
a train, and a ship

a necklace, a watch,
a belt, and a bag

HOST A POP-STAR CONTEST

Are you ready for some all-singing, all-dancing fun?
Invite friends and family to join in as judges, performers,
and audience members, and shine like a star.

Start by choosing the perfect place for performances—you'll need a doorway for stylish entrances, a "stage" area with plenty of room for performers to show their best moves, and a space opposite for the judges to sit. Don't forget to leave some space for your audience.

BACKSTAGE PASSES

You also need a "backstage" area for the performers to prepare—your bedroom would be ideal. They will need room to change into their costumes, mirrors to check their star-style make-up, space to practice their moves, and drinks and snacks to help them relax.

JUST JUDGING

Parents and grandparents make the perfect contest judges. Persuade up to four of them to join in and prepare a score sheet for each person with a column for each of the categories shown below. Categories are scored out of ten, with a total score out of 50:

Name	Styling	Singing	Dancing	Interview	Total

A WINNING PERFORMANCE!

Contestants need to put on the best possible show for the judges. Here's how to get an outstanding score in each category:

Name:

Lots of well-known performers have stage names. For instance, Sandra Smith is a lovely name, but Sandrine Star is definitely a 10-out-of-10 superstar name. Come up with your own to really impress the judges.

Styling:

The judges must score each act on her overall costume—including her outfit, hair, and makeup, if used. Try to choose outfits with as much sparkle as possible. Shiny fabrics will stand out particularly well. Add glittery make-up if you have any, and make your hair as gorgeous as possible.

Singing and Dancing:

Remember to choose a song you are familiar with so you don't forget the words. Dance routines should be kept simple so you don't get too out of breath to sing! The judges will still be wowed as long as you keep moving.

Interview:

The judges should ask each contestant a series of questions about her performance. Plan some answers in advance to avoid going blank, and remember to look the judges in the eyes.

Hint. The judges should reveal the top three scores in reverse order for maximum suspense. The winner closes the contest with a final performance of her winning song.

PARTY PERFECTION

Invite some friends over, put on some Christmas music, and have the best Christmas party ever! Here's how . . .

HUMAN CHRISTMAS TREE

This is a fun, fast game to test your friends' creativity. Here's how to play it . . .

1. Gather up all the gift wrap, ribbons, tinsel, and ornaments you can find and divide them into two equal piles.

2. Split your guests into two teams and decide which player on each team is going to be the human Christmas tree.

3. Each team has five minutes to decorate their player. As the host, you get to decide which team has done the best job.

SNOWBALL OLYMPICS

There'll be marshmallow madness when this game begins!

1. Decorate two large bowls with garland and place them at one end of the room.

2. Split your guests into two teams and give each player three marshmallows.

3. Ask players to stand about 6 feet back from the bowls. Each player must throw as many marshmallows as they can into their bowl.

The team that gets the most marshmallows into their bowl wins.

Ask your guests to write messages in this box.

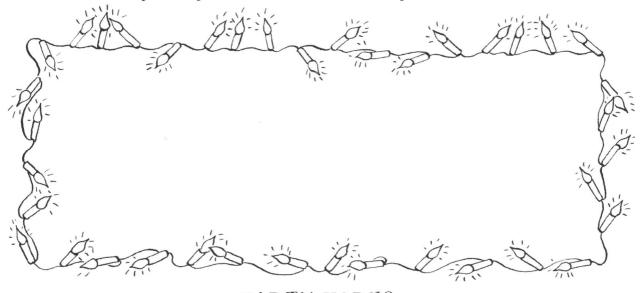

PARTY HORNS

Set up a craft table so your guests can make their own
cool party horns. Here's how . . .

You will need:

- lots of strips of gift wrap,
  measuring 2 in. x 8 in.
- drinking straws cut into
  2 in. lengths • tape

What you do:

1. Fold a strip of gift wrap lengthways into three and use tape to seal the side and one of the ends.

2. Starting at the sealed end, roll the paper up.

3. Put a piece of straw into the open end of the paper and use tape to hold it in place. Make sure there are no gaps between the straw and the top of the paper.

4. Blow into the straw. Ta da!

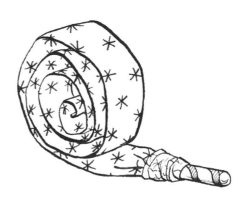

GLAM UP YOUR GIFTS

Want an easy way to give your gift wrap the "wow" factor?
Check out these cool ideas to make sure your presents really stand out.

PRETTY PAPERS

To achieve this simple, yet sophisticated look, first wrap each present in a single color of gift wrap—the brighter the better.

Next, cut a wide strip of pretty, patterned paper in a contrasting color that fits around the gift, leaving just a bit of the plain paper showing on either side.

Finally, tie a thin ribbon around the middle of the patterned strip for the perfect finishing touch to your seriously glamorous gifts.

THINK OUTSIDE THE BOX

Tired of store-bought gift wrap? Get creative and think of other materials you could use to wrap your gifts and make them really original. Here are some ideas to get you started:

- Wrap a framed holiday photo in a map of the place where it was taken.

- Tie shampoos and bubble baths into a luxury bundle using a bright headscarf.

- Cover CDs or concert tickets in sheet music for an extra-funky feel.

RADICAL RIBBONS

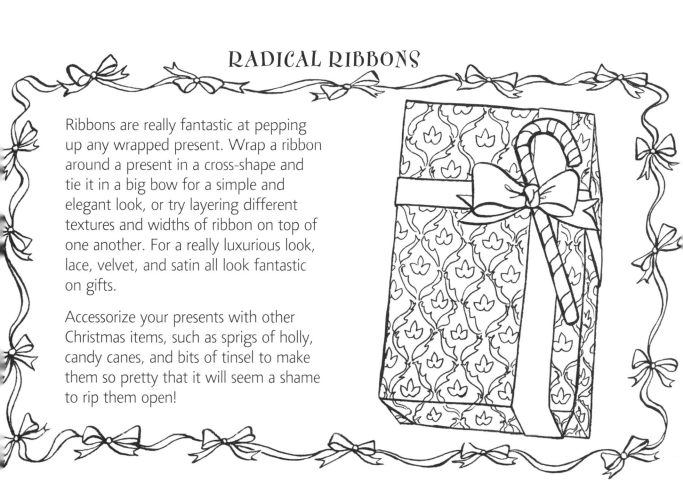

Ribbons are really fantastic at pepping up any wrapped present. Wrap a ribbon around a present in a cross-shape and tie it in a big bow for a simple and elegant look, or try layering different textures and widths of ribbon on top of one another. For a really luxurious look, lace, velvet, and satin all look fantastic on gifts.

Accessorize your presents with other Christmas items, such as sprigs of holly, candy canes, and bits of tinsel to make them so pretty that it will seem a shame to rip them open!

Make these gifts gorgeous with paper, bows, and ribbons.

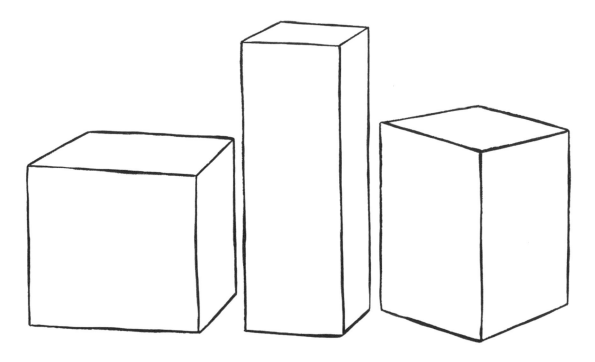

SUPER SLEIGH DASH

It's Christmas Eve and Santa has asked you and your friends to help him to deliver the presents!

Place a coin for each player on the start line at Santa's headquarters, then race off in your sleigh. The first to deliver the presents to the house at the end is the winner.

Reindeer need feeding. Miss a turn.

Rudolph knows a shortcut. Jump ahead.

BRAZIL

ITALY

You misread the map. Move back 4 spaces.

You skid on a patch of ice. Move forward 2 spaces.

EGYPT

FRANCE

Miss a turn waiting for the children to fall asleep.

FINISH

HOLLAND

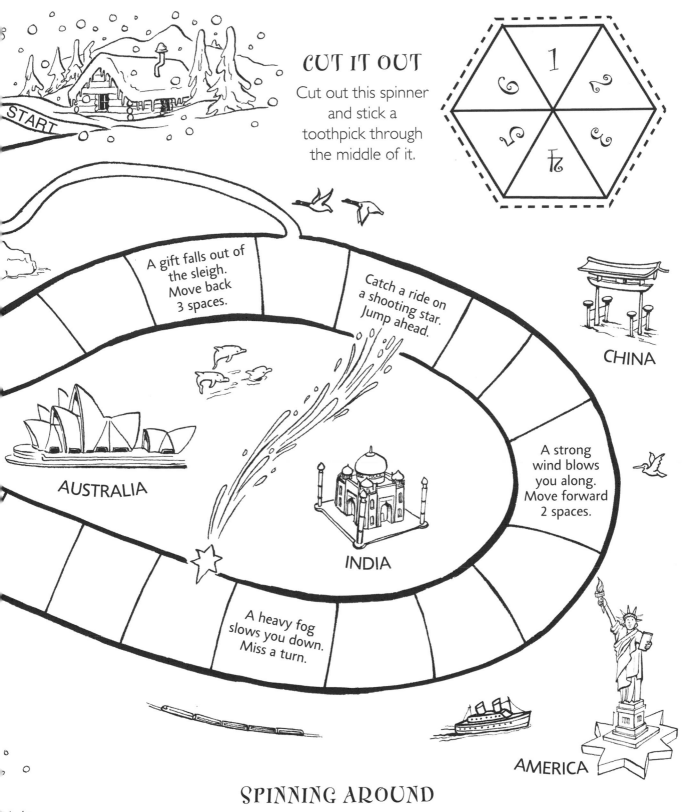

CUT IT OUT

Cut out this spinner and stick a toothpick through the middle of it.

START

A gift falls out of the sleigh. Move back 3 spaces.

Catch a ride on a shooting star. Jump ahead.

CHINA

AUSTRALIA

A strong wind blows you along. Move forward 2 spaces.

INDIA

A heavy fog slows you down. Miss a turn.

AMERICA

SPINNING AROUND

To spin your spinner, hold the toothpick upright between your finger and thumb, and twist so that the spinner spins. The number that is at the top of the spinner when it stops tells you the number of spaces you should move your coin.

Fill the page with snowflakes.

CHRISTMAS BASKETS

Your school has put together some Christmas food baskets for people in need. Can you deliver them to the following locations on the map?

1. D4   **2.** C2   **3.** A3   **4.** E1   **5.** B4

These numbers and letters are called coordinates. To use them, place your finger on the letter given. Move along the row to the column that matches the number. In that square you will find the symbol the coordinate refers to. Use the key to work out where each basket needs to go. Check your answers on page 95.

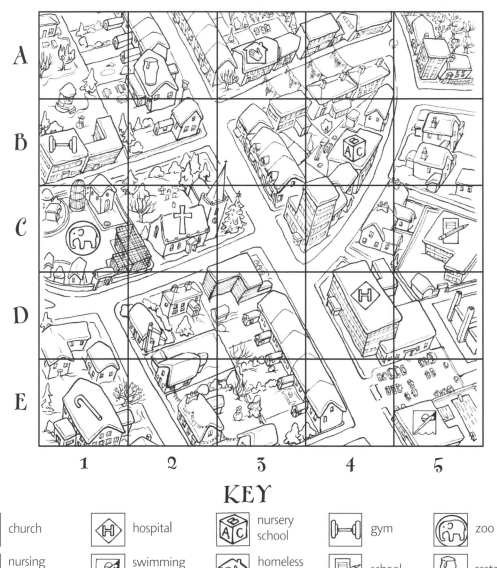

KEY

✝ church	Ⓗ hospital	🅰🅱🅲 nursery school	gym	🐘 zoo
nursing home	swimming pool	homeless shelter	school	restaurant

CHRISTMAS DAY MEMORIES

Make sure you remember the wonderful things that happened over Christmas by answering these questions before the Christmas holiday is over.

What did you do on
Christmas Eve?

Are there any traditions that your family
follows every Christmas?

Who did you spend
Christmas Day with?

What was the funniest thing
that happened?

What did you have to eat on
Christmas Day? Draw it on this plate.

What did you wear on Christmas Day?
Draw your outfit on this girl.

Which Christmas present did you like
the best? Draw a picture of it here.

GIFT RECORD

Complete this gift record as you open your presents so that you
remember who to send thank-you cards to!

NAME	GIFT

SAY THANK YOU

Homemade cards to say thank you for Christmas presents are much more personal than a thank-you e-mail, and this extra-special card is sure to be treasured forever. Here's how to make it . . .

You will need:

• 2 pieces of 8 ½ x 11 in. card stock • crayons • small piece of the gift wrap that the gift came in • scissors • glue • putty • pencil • string

What you do:

1. Fold one of the pieces of card stock in half and place it in front of you so that the fold is along the top.

2. Draw a picture of the person who gave you the gift on the left of the card, and a picture of you with your arms out to receive it on the right.

3. Unfold your card. You need to make two holes in the card—one next to the hands of the person that gave you the gift and one next to your own hands. The easiest way to do this is to place the front of the card over a piece of putty

and carefully push a pencil through the card and into the putty.

4. Cut a small gift-shape out of the gift wrap. Glue it on to the second piece of card and cut it out.

5. Cut a piece of string a bit longer than the width of the card.

6. Poke a hole in the center of the gift using the method from step **3** and thread the string through the hole.

7. Pop the ends of the string through the holes on the front of the card. Knot it on the back so that it can't be pulled through. You will now be able to move the gift along the string.

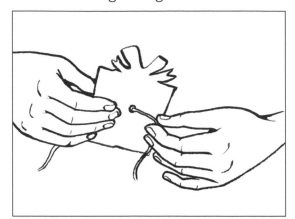

Handy Writing Hints

Now that you've made your gorgeous card, it's time to write inside it. Here's how to write a terrific thank you . . .

Dear ------------------,

First, thank him or her for the gift and try to use an adjective to describe it, for example, "Thank you so much for the delicious chocolates / beautiful scarf / interesting book."

Then say something about why you like the gift or how you plan to use it. For example, "I am wearing the pajamas as I write this—they are so warm and cozy I don't want to take them off!"

Next say something personal, such as, "It was great to see you over Christmas, and I laugh every time I think of that game of charades! I can't wait for a rematch."

Finally, sign off with another thank you, "Thanks again for such a thoughtful gift. You are so good at choosing presents."

With love,

------------------ xxx

DICE DECIDER

Can't decide what to do on the days between Christmas and the start of school? Make this dice activity decider to help you choose!

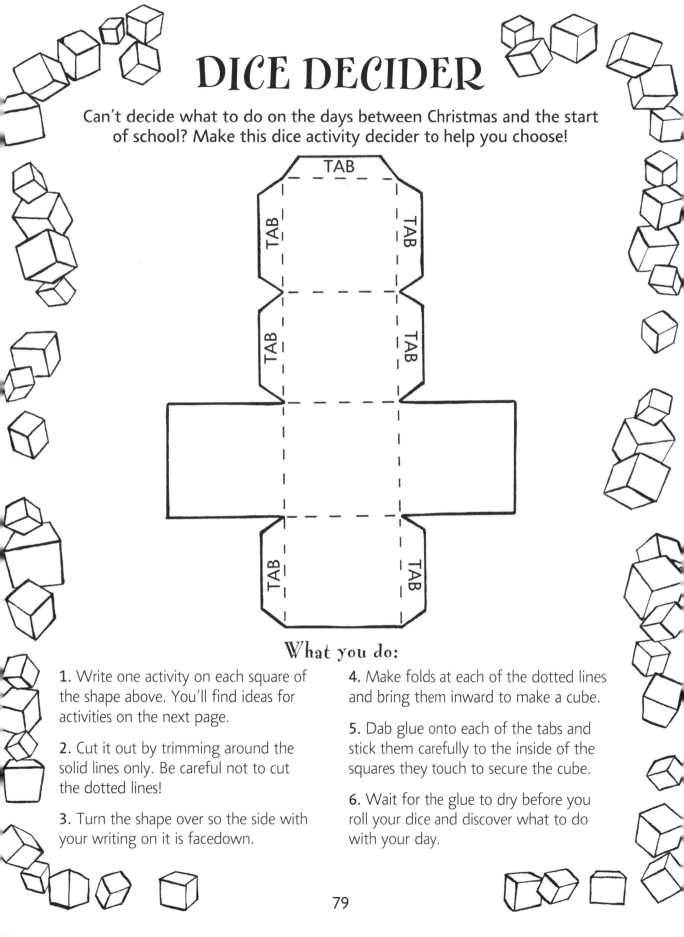

TAB

TAB

TAB

TAB

TAB

TAB

TAB

TAB

What you do:

1. Write one activity on each square of the shape above. You'll find ideas for activities on the next page.

2. Cut it out by trimming around the solid lines only. Be careful not to cut the dotted lines!

3. Turn the shape over so the side with your writing on it is facedown.

4. Make folds at each of the dotted lines and bring them inward to make a cube.

5. Dab glue onto each of the tabs and stick them carefully to the inside of the squares they touch to secure the cube.

6. Wait for the glue to dry before you roll your dice and discover what to do with your day.

GET INSPIRED

Here are some suggestions for activities to write on the squares of your dice. Use these, or get creative and come up with some of your own.

Make a family "newspaper" about your Christmas holiday.

Create a sculpture from all the boxes and leftover gift wrap.

Write your thank-you cards.

Make up a Christmas play and perform it for your family.

Make a treasure hunt for your friends.

Play Christmas-themed charades.

CRAZY CHRISTMAS JOKES

What did the big snowman say to the little snowman?
Can you smell carrots?

What goes, "Oh, oh, oh!"?
Santa walking backward.

What do angry mice send to one another at Christmas?
Cross-mouse cards.

What happens if you eat Christmas decorations?
You get tinsel-itus!

Give the reindeer twisty antlers.

TWELVE DAYS OF CHRISTMAS CALENDAR

Christmas isn't just one day—it's twelve! Traditionally, Christmas starts on December 25 and goes until January 6. Celebrate every day of the holidays with this special calendar.

You will need:

- Christmas gift wrap • scissors • glue • gold marker
- 40 in. length of ribbon or string • tape • clothespins
- small goodies (see next page for ideas)

What you do:

1. Cut a square of gift wrap, measuring 8 in. x 8 in. and place it with the patterned side down and one of the corners facing you.

2. Fold the corner on the left and the corner on the right inward so that they meet in the middle of the square.

3. Fold up the bottom corner so that it overlaps with the folds at the sides as shown below. Crease firmly. This will be the bottom of your envelope.

4. Unfold the envelope, then fold the bottom corner up to meet the creased line that you have just made.

5. Fold the bottom of the envelope up again along the original crease, and fold the sides back into the middle on top of the folded bottom flap.

6. Turn the top of each side flap down a little, creating a corner where they meet the bottom flap as shown below.

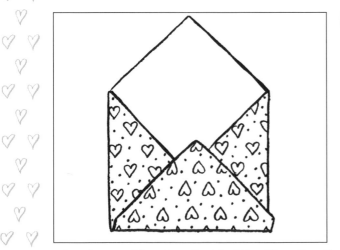
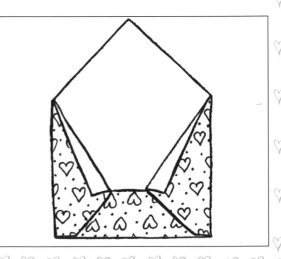

7. Unfold the sides of the envelope and fold the paper back in along the creases you have just made so that the pattern shows on the inside.

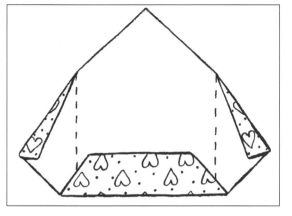

8. Fold the sides in again, and tuck each of the folds inside the bottom of the envelope. Crease and secure with glue.

9. Fold down the top flap to just below where the side flaps start and tuck it into the pocket you have created.

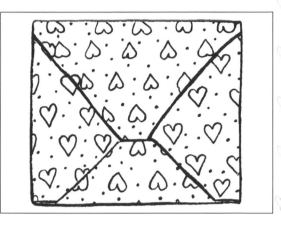

10. Repeat steps **1** to **9** to make eleven more envelopes.

ON THE FIRST DAY OF CHRISTMAS . . .

Now that you've made the envelopes, it's time to turn them into a special Twelve Days of Christmas calendar and keep Christmas going. Here's how . . .

1. Use the gold marker to number the envelopes 1 to 12 on the front where you would usually write an address.

2. Fill the envelopes with goodies. You could include a Christmas joke, an idea for a challenge to be completed that day, or a foil-wrapped chocolate.

3. Stick the ribbon or string along a wall with tape so that it is stretched out horizontally.

4. Use the clothespins to hang the envelopes in a line along the ribbon.

5. Starting on December 25, open one envelope each day and enjoy the goodies inside.

RELAX TO THE MAX

A Christmas vacation is the perfect opportunity to wind down and de-stress. Spend some time looking after your mind and body with these relaxation techniques. Choose from the following, or make a day of it and do them all!

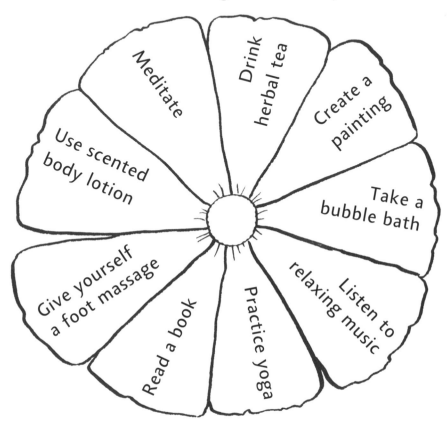

- Meditate
- Drink herbal tea
- Create a painting
- Use scented body lotion
- Take a bubble bath
- Give yourself a foot massage
- Read a book
- Practice yoga
- Listen to relaxing music

MEDITATION STATION

Meditation is a great way to help you feel calmer and more relaxed. Here's how to get started:

1. Sit cross-legged on the floor.

2. Concentrate on your breathing and take ten long, deep breaths. When you breathe in, imagine peace and calm entering your body, and when you breathe out, imagine all the tension leaving your body.

3. Continue to breathe deeply and evenly, but now focus your mind on all the good things in your life. Think about the people you love and the things you enjoy doing. This will help you to feel calm, happy, and full of energy.

4. Finish with five more long, deep breaths.

5. Write down any ideas or thoughts that came to you during your meditation in a notebook.

SIX-STEP YOGA

As well as making you feel more relaxed, yoga is a great way to stretch your muscles and improve your flexibility. Try holding each pose in this series for a minute and see how you feel.

1. Lie flat on your back with your palms facing the ceiling.

2. Hug your knees to your chest.

3. Sit up and stretch your legs out in front of you. Place your hands on the floor at your sides. Gently bend your neck and tilt your head forward toward your chest.

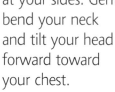

4. Stand up. Stretch your arms up above your head and press the palms of your hands together.

5. Raise one foot off the ground and rest it against the side of your other leg. Repeat with the other foot.

6. Lastly, shake your body out like this.

PARTY PUZZLERS

It's party time! Complete these puzzles, then turn to page 95
to check your answers.

VIP PARTY CODE

This party is so top secret that even the invitation has been written in code.

Move each letter two letters backward in the alphabet to work out where the party is and what time it starts.

For example, if the letter "c" appears on the invitation, replace it with an "a."

Eqog vq Jqnna Jcnn qp
Ejtkuvocu Tqcf cv jcnh
rcuv gkijv.

LET'S DANCE

A. How many girls have at least one arm in the air?

B. How many are wearing belts?

C. How many have stars somewhere on their outfits?

D. How many are wearing ballet flats?

What has Santa given the girls at the Christmas party?

SLEEPOVER PUZZLERS

The girls are having a Christmas vacation sleepover, so grab a pen and test your skills! Can you find your way through the maze to get to the sleepover on time? On the way, you need to pick up your friends Katie and Jessie. You'll find the answers on page 96.

Katie

SLEEPOVER
MYSTERY
MAZE

Jessie

ROBE MIX-UP

Can you figure out which robe belongs to which girl?
You can find the answers on page 95.

Jenny   Jo   Kim   Katie

SNACK TIME!

The girls are having pizza for their midnight feast. Two of them have chosen identical slices—can you spot which two are identical?

MIDDLE-NAME LOGIC

The girls are trying to guess one another's middle names. Can you give them a helping hand? Write the correct first name next to the middle names below using the following clues:

1. Jenny's middle name starts with an *S*.

2. Jo's middle name has an *L* in it.

3. Kim's middle name is not the longest.

4. Katie's name is as long as Jenny's.

. . . . Isabelle

. . . . Coral

. . . . Sophie

. . . . Sarah

SNOWY DAY SCIENTIST

Roll up your sleeves and turn your kitchen into a laboratory with these excellent experiments.

SUPER SUGAR ROCKS

In this experiment, you can make your own scientific sugar lollipop from a "supersaturated" solution of sugar.

You will need:

- an empty glass jar with a lid
- a piece of string, 6 in. long
- a bag of white sugar

Warning: Always ask an adult to help you when you use the stove.

Sugar is a substance that is soluble in a liquid. This means that when it is added to water, it dissolves. The water becomes sugary, and there are no sugar granules left. The liquid is now a solution. There's a limit to how much sugar can be dissolved in a glass of water, though, and when this limit is reached, the solution is saturated.

However, there's something you can do to get more sugar into a solution: add heat.

To see this in action, ask an adult to help you boil water and then fill your jar with it. The jar will be hot, so ask the adult to hold it steady for you with an oven mitt.

Now it's time to add the sugar. See if

you can guess how many teaspoons of sugar will dissolve in the hot water. Add a spoonful at a time and stir until it dissolves.

When no more sugar will dissolve, lower your piece of string into the water so that the end hangs over the rim of the jar. Trap it with the jar lid, and leave the jar in a safe place.

As the solution cools, the extra sugar will not be able to stay dissolved, and sugar crystals will start to form on the string.

After a week, you will have a delicious sugar lollipop! Yum.

SHE'S ELECTRIC!

Use this experiment to create your own static electricity.

You will need:

• a plastic comb • running water

Everything in the world is made of atoms—tiny particles that are too small to see. Inside each atom, there are even smaller particles: protons, neutrons, and electrons. Protons have a positive electrical charge. Neutrons are neutral—they have no charge. Electrons are negatively charged.

Most of the time, atoms have no charge. However, if you rub two objects together, you can create a charge that makes the electrons move from one atom to another. This charge is static electricity.

To do this yourself, simply run your comb through your hair a few times. This will make negatively charged electrons jump from your hair to the comb. The comb will now have a negative charge.

Now run a very thin stream of water and hold the charged comb close to it. The water will be attracted to the comb and "bend" toward it!

SOAP-TASTIC!

Discover how gas expands when heated with this incredible experiment.

You will need:

• a bar of soap • a microwave
• a microwaveable bowl

Warning: Make sure you ask an adult for help with the microwave in this experiment.

Note: A bar of soap that has lots of tiny air bubbles in it—one that floats in the bath, for example—will work best for this experiment.

Remove any stickers from the soap and place it in the bowl in the microwave. Heat for two minutes on full power, watching all the time to see what happens. As the soap gets hotter, the gas inside the bubbles—air—expands and the solid bar of soap will foam up out of the bowl. Amazing!

Allow the soap to cool for at least five minutes before you touch it. Clean the microwave before anyone cooks food in it.

ALL THE ANSWERS

PUZZLE WORKSHOP
pages 6 and 7

There are 19 elves making mischief in Santa's workshop.

Reindeer **B** and **E** are identical.

GET YOUR SKATES ON
page 11

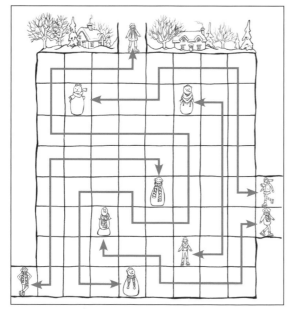

WISH UPON A STAR
page 13

CHRISTMAS QUIZ
pages 14 and 15

1. D 2. A 3. A 4. C

5. B 6. D 7. C 8. A

9. B 10. C.

CHRISTMAS SHOPPING CHAOS
page 18

TRICKY TRACKS
page 30

1 is Comet

2 is Prancer

3 is Cupid

4 is Dancer

5 is Dasher

BRAIN BOGGLERS
pages 32 and 33

Trophy Time
Alex has three trophies. Here's why: If Alex had won 'at least five' trophies, then Alyssa and Emily would both be right as that is 'more than one'. If he had won an even number of trophies, as Preeya says, Emily would also be right as that is always more than one. Emily's is the only answer that can be right when the other girls' answers are wrong.

Sunflower Sums
Because the sunflower doubles in height every day, and is as tall as her after 30 days, it will be half her height the day before, after 29 days.

Summer Fun
The fourth child is Summer!

Donkey Dilemma

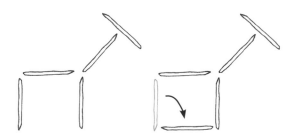

Chocolate Conundrum

If Rebecca removes a chocolate from the box marked "Milk and White Chocolate," the solution is simple.

All of the labels are wrong, so the box marked "Milk and White Chocolate" must contain either milk or white chocolate. If Rebecca gets a milk chocolate, then that box must contain only milk chocolates. This means that the box that is marked "White Chocolate" must be the mixed box and the remaining box should have the "White Chocolate" label.

Who's the Top?

Louisa is 105 cm (3 ft 5 in) tall.
Siân 100 cm (3 ft 3 in) tall.
Sally 115 cm (3 ft 9 in) tall.
Preeya 110 cm (3 ft 7 in) tall.

MAJOR MIX-UP
page 41

The missing pieces of the jigsaw puzzle are **B**, **C** and **E**.

WHITE CHRISTMAS
pages 48 and 49

Girl **B** has hit Aunt Sally with her snowball. Oops!

Lydia's snowman is snowman **B**.

TRUE OR FALSE
page 52

Ukrainians believe that finding a spider's web on Christmas Eve is good luck. **TRUE**

Italian children are brought gifts by a friendly witch, as well as Santa Claus. **TRUE**

In Brazil, Santa wears red and white shorts so that he can enjoy the summer heat. **FALSE** – but he does wear silk clothing to keep him cool.

Spanish children play on swings at Christmas, to tell the sun to "swing" high in the sky over the coming year. **TRUE**

At Christmas time, Swedish boys dress up as holly sprigs in green clothes and red hats. **FALSE** – they dress up as stars in long, white shirts and pointed hats.

In Australia, Santa arrives on the back of a kangaroo. **FALSE** – but he sometimes arrives on a surfboard!

COOKIE MIX-UP
page 58

1. Peace
2. Joy
3. Party
4. Merry
5. Festive
6. Smile
7. Wish
8. Happy

PUPPY POWER!
page 60

Puppy **A** belongs to Rosie.
Puppy **B** belongs to Leila.
Puppy **C** belongs to Caitlin.

SHOP SUDOKU
page 63

CHRISTMAS BASKETS
page 73

1 is the hospital.
2 is the church.
3 is the homeless shelter.
4 is the nursing home.
5 is the nursery.

PARTY PUZZLERS
pages 86 and 87

The coded party invitation says:
Come to Holly Hall on Christmas Road at half past eight.

Let's Dance

A. Five girls have at least one arm in the air.
B. Three girls are wearing belts.
C. Five girls have stars on their outfits.
D. Three girls are wearing ballet pumps.

SLEEPOVER PUZZLER
pages 88 and 89

Sleepover Mystery Maze

Robe Mix-Up
Dressing gown **C** belongs to Jenny.
Dressing gown **D** belongs to Jo.
Dressing gown **A** belongs to Kim.
Dressing gown **B** belongs to Katie.

Snack Time!
C and **D** are the matching pizza slices.

Middle-Name Logic
Jo's middle name is Isabelle.
Katie's middle name is Coral.
Kim's middle name is Sophie.
Jenny's middle name is Sarah.